Step into Fall
A New Season

by Jane Belk Moncure
illustrated by Susan Lexa-Senning

Created by  THE CHILDS WORLD

Distributed by CHILDRENS PRESS®
Chicago, Illinois

Grateful appreciation is expressed to Elizabeth Hammerman, Ed. D., Science Education Specialist, for her services as consultant.

CHILDRENS PRESS HARDCOVER EDITION
ISBN 0-516-08124-1

CHILDRENS PRESS PAPERBACK EDITION
ISBN 0-516-48124-X

Library of Congress Cataloging in Publication Data

Moncure, Jane Belk.
    Step into fall : a new season / by Jane Belk Moncure ; illustrated by Susan Lexa-Senning ; created by Child's World.
    p. cm. — (Discovery world)
    Summary: Describes the various aspects of autumn in brief text and illustrations.
    ISBN 0-89565-573-X
    1. Autumn—Juvenile literature.   2. Natural history—Juvenile literature.   [1. Autumn.]   I. Lexa-Senning, Susan, ill.   II. Child's World (Firm)   III. Title.   IV. Series.
QH81.M739   1990
574.5'43—dc20   90-30637
                                                                   CIP
                                                                   AC

©1990 The Child's World, Inc.
Elgin, IL

1 2 3 4 5 6 7 8 9 10 11 12 R 99 98 97 96 95 94 93 92 91 90

Step into Fall
A New Season

Where is Discovery World?
It can be anywhere—
anywhere at all.
It can be at a zoo,
a museum, or beside the sea.
It can be in a pond,
a library, or up in a tree.
All you need is curiosity.
It can be right at
your own back door.
All you need to do is EXPLORE!

Fall is here. How can you tell? Button up
your sweater and let's take a walk through
fall.

Here we go!

You can tell fall is here because the leaves on the trees are turning red, yellow, and pumpkin orange. They are falling all around.

Jump into a big bunch of crispy, crunchy leaves. Down you go, just like a falling leaf!

9

Leaves are not the only things falling this
time of year. Acorns are falling from the
oak tree. Frisky squirrels are busy picking
them up.

The squirrels get ready for winter by burying their acorns in the ground. On snowy days, when food is hard to find, the squirrels will dig up their treasure.

11

Other animals are storing food for winter
too. "Tap, tap, tap." A red-headed
woodpecker stuffs a fat acorn under the
bark of a tree.

There goes a chipmunk! Her cheeks are puffed with seeds and nuts. She will hide them in her underground home.

Some animals get ready for winter by
getting fat! The woodchuck eats and eats
until he is very plump.

Then he squeezes into his den, curls up,
and closes his eyes. He will not eat again
until spring.

Listen! Do you hear the wild geese? Look
up in the sky. There goes a flock of geese.

They are flying south to spend winter in
a warmer place. There they will have no
trouble finding food.

Not all animals travel south for winter.
Many animals stay close by. The little box
turtle digs under ground and stays there
until spring.

The woolly bear caterpillar hides in the
leaves. He curls up in a little, fuzzy ball
and stays under the leaves until spring.

Slowly, the chilly days of fall grow colder
and shorter. One day frost covers the
ground. The wildflowers in the field have
all turned brown. And look! The milkweed
pods have burst wide open.

Blow the fluffy, white seeds into the air.
Away they go, floating like tiny parachutes
in the wind. Next spring some of the seeds
will sprout and grow into new plants.

Now it is time for the farmer to gather his
pumpkins. It is time for jack-o-lanterns and
pumpkin pies.

The apples are ripe and ready for the
market. It is time for applesauce and
apple jelly.

The farm pony likes apples too. Feed her
an apple and feel her thick fur. She has
grown a warm coat for the snowy days
ahead.

The sheep have grown warm, wooly coats
for winter too. Already, icy winds are
blowing.

Soon the days are so short that darkness
comes before dinnertime. It is so cold, ice
is beginning to cover the pond. Fall is
coming to an end.

One morning, the sky looks goose-feather gray. Suddenly, snowflakes fill the air. Run and get your sled. What new season is about to begin?

EXPLORE SOME MORE WITH PROFESSOR FACTO!

Ask an adult to help you find where you live on a globe. Do you live on the top half of the world or on the bottom half? Did you know that when it is fall on the top half of the world, it is spring on the bottom half?

For the top half of the world, fall begins around September 22. It ends around December 22. Use a calendar to find out how many weeks are in fall. What holidays come in fall? Is your birthday in fall?

Here is a delicious fall treat you can make with applesauce. It is called **apple leather**. You will need an adult to help you.

1. Ask an adult to preheat the oven to 400°.

2. Grease a cookie sheet by rubbing butter onto it with a paper towel.

3. Pour just a little bit of applesauce at a time onto the cookie sheet. Spread the applesauce around so that it just barely covers the bottom of the pan. It should be ⅛ inch or 3 millimeters thick.

4. Ask an adult to put the pan in the oven and turn the temperature down to 180°. Cook the applesauce for about 3 hours, until the apple leather can be peeled from the pan.

5. Ask an adult to take the pan out of the oven and let it cool. Use clean scissors to cut the apple leather into pieces.

YUM!

OIC 2

Fall is a good time to go on a leaf hunt.
Take a walk through a forest. Collect as
many different kinds of leaves as you can
find. When you are done, sort your leaves
into groups. First sort them by color. How
many colors did you find?

Now look at the edges of each leaf. Are
the edges smooth, like this?

Or do they have jagged points, like this?

Or do they look like they have big bites
taken out of them, like this?

Sort the leaves according to what kinds of
edges they have. Which group has the
most leaves?

Now hold each leaf up to the light. Do you see lines on the leaf? Those are called **veins**. They carry food and water to the leaf. Look at the pattern of the veins on each leaf.

How many leaves look like this, with one thick vein down the middle and thinner veins going out on either side?

How many leaves look like this, with several thick veins that go out from the stem?

When you are through examing your leaves, you can make **leaf creatures** with them. Just glue the leaves down on paper and draw heads, arms, and legs around them with crayons or markers.

31

INDEX